# STARVING YOUR FEARS

*From Panic to Peace in 10 Easy Steps*

## Joyce E. Logan, Ph.D.

*Metaphysical Philosophy*

# The Story of Two Wolves

*An old Cherokee is teaching his grandson about life.*
*"A fight is going on inside me," he said to the boy.*

*"It is a terrible fight and it is between two wolves.*
*One is evil – he is anger, envy, sorrow, regret, greed,*
*arrogance, self-pity, guilt, resentment, inferiority,*
*lies, false pride, superiority, and ego."*

*He continued, "The other is good – he is joy, peace,*
*love, hope, serenity, humility, kindness, benevolence,*
*empathy, generosity, truth, compassion, and*
*faith. The same fight is going on inside you – and*
*inside every other person, too."*

*The grandson thought about it for a minute and then*
*asked his grandfather, "Which wolf will win?"*

*The old Cherokee simply replied, "The one you feed."*

**The one you "starve" will fade away... I will show**
**you how to do that.**

# Acknowledgements

First and foremost; I dedicate this book to my mother, Ann Ottenbreit Carrano, who taught me and then showed me what true courage was on a daily basis.

To everyone I have had the honor of working with and helping them through and out of their anxiety and panic attacks – you are truly my heroes! I could not have written this book without your honesty.

Lastly and lovingly; my husband and photographer extraordinaire, Wayne Logan, who not only took all the photos in this book; but also encouraged me every step of the way through many difficult and magnificent journeys. These are the last photos he took before Alzheimer's erased most of his memories including his passion for photography. However, it didn't rob him of his smile nor sweet nature.

Forever grateful – I love you all!

# About the Author

Joyce is a motivational speaker and a self-proclaimed recovering anxiety addict.

She holds a Doctorate in metaphysical philosophy from The American Institute of Holistic Theology in Youngstown, OH and is a Certified Hypnotherapist from The National Guild of Hypnotists in NH. She also founded *"The Wellness Center"* in Connecticut, which she presided over for many years. She has written columns in various magazines about overcoming fears and relaxation techniques.

Due to her down to earth manner, she is a sought after speaker, radio & TV guest. Joyce is most passionate about this book as it's partly about her own life, her mother's struggle with panic attacks and agoraphobia, and inspiring stories of those she personally worked with and helped overcome their fears. People have asked her for years to write a book so they could keep her words nearby or pass on to others; and this is it!

# CONTENTS

*I keep the telephone of my mind open to peace, harmony, health, love and abundance. Then, whenever doubt, anxiety or fear try to call me, they keep getting a busy signal – and soon they'll forget my number.*

**Edith Armstrong**

# Introduction

I cannot remember a time when I wasn't afraid of something... from the proverbial "Boogie Man" under my bed to the moon falling from the sky and ending the world, which would also mean my inevitable falling into the bowels of hell, where torture never ends. Never! I have nine years of Catholic schooling to thank for that one. But nothing could prepare me for the debilitating panic attacks that gradually crept into my life. Those swift and unexpected attacks struck my body like flashes of lightning, completely robbing me of the peace and joy I should have been experiencing in my life, especially during my 20's and 30's. How many times had I heard my peers, relatives, and even therapists tell me to "get over it" or to "try not to think about it"? Countless! They were all well-meaning, but sometimes I just wanted to scream, "If I could just get over this, don't you think I would in a heartbeat?"

My mother suffered with agoraphobia for 30 years. Agoraphobia means fear of wide-open spaces. The Greek root "agora" means "public open space" and "marketplace." Therefore, agoraphobia is also the fear of crowds such as being in theaters, grocery stores, boarding a plane or even standing in line; it's anyplace where they will feel trapped and helpless.

They also fear fleeing the situation as they'll be embarrassed, not knowing what to tell others. This type of fear causes very physical reactions; heart racing, dizziness, sweating, and can even mimic symptoms of a heart attack. This reaction can be so overwhelming that many are unable to leave their homes to avoid going through that experience ever again!

As a child, I never heard her speak about it. I'm sure she must have thought she was going mad, and no one spoke openly about mental illness in those days. I only knew that she didn't like to be alone: I could hear the panic in her voice when we went for rides or when my dad drove over a bridge or, worse yet, planned a trip to Florida! No one knew how my mother agonized over leaving the safety of her home, fearing that she'd have an attack of "something"... something that no one could quite understand or explain to her. Being that I was just a kid, I paid little attention to what was happening. My mother worked hard at submersing her fears through cooking, and her baking resulting in an abundance of homemade pizzas, stews, fruit pies, cakes, delectable cookies and pastries, all made from scratch! There can be a positive side to anxiety disorders for others in the family, but it sure doesn't feel that way to the person who experiences them.

Although I had many fears, the real culprit, the big anxiety attack, didn't hit me full force till I was in my early 20's. Married with two small boys, I can still recall that moment when my life changed forever.

I was grocery shopping, and as I walked down to the far end of the store I thought I felt the earth shift. Shocked and confused, I couldn't understand why no one else seemed to notice that the store was tilting! Then, in one of those moments of glaring insight, I realized... nothing was wrong with the store, it was me! The floor seemed crooked, my heart began to race, and I was flooded with fear. It would be years before I entered a major supermarket again.

For years following that first incident, I walked through life as if my knees were plowing through thick mud. I was always anticipating the next big attack. I couldn't wait to get out of ANY store, the hairdresser's, the elevator. My list grew longer with each passing month. I became a master of deception. I had other people pick up my groceries or my kids at school. Soon my marriage fell apart, and no one noticed that I needed help. I managed to hide it all with lipstick and a smile. I could conceal a boatload of sins by putting on some makeup. No one would suspect that death felt imminent, and that I was dying inside.

My life was fading away, slipping out of my grasp, while I was locked in a shrinking world.

What do you do when your panic attacks start happening at home? Where do you run? By now, I knew about agoraphobia. Dr. Claire Weeks wrote a wonderful book called *"Hope and Help for Your Nerves"*. At last, a book about these attacks, this monster that had possessed my body. I joined a group of like-minded folks who had generalized anxiety disorder or full blown panic attacks, and, for a while, I watched while they seemed to get better and move on... leaving me behind. The group's leader told us that we were struggling with "panic disorder" or "agoraphobia," and many people seemed to get better almost instantaneously just knowing that they weren't going crazy and that these feelings had a name! But, I already knew the name and what I was dealing with, after living through it with my mother. It had a name, it was a disorder, and yet, nothing changed for me. I still had bouts of hyperventilation, a racing heart, numbness, and tingling in my hands. Each headache was certain to be a brain tumor or an aneurysm.

I have been on a long journey, trying to find the road to peace. I've gone through it all, short of actually drinking "snake oil" but did drink the weirdest concoction which caused me to break out in a rash from head to toe to drinking brandy (a bit too much), and seeing psychics who weren't so psychic: Bowel cleansing, behavioral therapy, and numerous medications. I had crystal powder placed in my nostrils, visited healers (who didn't seem that healthy) and poured out my heart to psychiatrists to no avail (one was even arrested for trying to kill his girlfriend with a butcher's knife...yikes)!

I am here to tell you about my experiences in overcoming anxiety, knowing that it may save you from charlatans and well-meaning people... who just don't understand! I hope to save you years of research – as I've been your human guinea pig!

By 1980 I had learned so much about panic disorders that I became a "Field Worker" for TERRAP, a California-based treatment center created by Dr. Hardy: TERRAP is an acronym for "territorial apprehension." Jane Miller, a brilliant psychotherapist and author, spearheaded the Connecticut group. My job was to accompany people during the tasks that caused them the most anxiety, such as riding in a car, taking a walk, or riding in an elevator. I asked them how intense their anxiety levels were, on a scale of one to ten (10 being the highest level on the panic meter, and one being a number that I've only known while asleep... maybe).

This course helped people... some could possibly say it cured them, and many others repeated it quite a few times. I began taking some psychology courses at a state college, and I would hold small classes in a church basement in my attempts at helping others, while still trying to grasp the disorder myself. Fifteen years later, I received a Doctorate in Metaphysical Philosophy, and soon become a certified, clinical hypnotherapist.

I've learned a lot through my experiences, and my hope is that this book will give you some tools to overcome your anxiety and maybe a few laughs along the way.

ooooo

*Live as you will wish to have lived when you are dying.*

**Christian Furchtegott Gellent**

*Be of good cheer.*
*Do not think of today's failures,*
*but of the success that may come tomorrow.*
*You have set yourselves a difficult task,*
*but you will succeed if you persevere;*
*and you will find a joy in overcoming obstacles.*

**Helen Keller**

# The Good News...

People who have chronic or occasional anxiety and/or panic attacks are often highly intelligent, passionate, caring, thoughtful, creative human beings. The wonderful, creative mind that causes your anxiety is the very one that will lead you on your road to fulfillment. You can lead a normal, joyful life. The best is yet to come!

# The Bad News...

Fear doesn't go away, nor does anxiety magically disappear. There are no magic wands to wave over you, but you're more powerful than you realize.

This little book can change your life! It is meant for you to read and reread over and over again. It's your bible for overcoming fear. People who are recovering from alcoholism or addiction go to meetings several times a week, sometimes for their entire lives. Spiritual leaders read their Bibles or listen to positive audio books to reinforce their faith, and you need to reinforce *your* wellness by understanding and accepting your body. Becoming mindful creates an extraordinary capacity to build a strong body, mind and spirit in ourselves. You will achieve this!

*In the end, it's not the years in your life that count. It's the life in your years.*

**Abraham Lincoln**

# CHAPTER I

# How to Starve Your Fears

*Thought is the sculptor who can create the person you want to be.*

*Henry David Thoreau*

# How Do You Starve Your Fears?

What you don't feed will eventually starve to death. It's a law of nature that applies to you, both physically and mentally.

**Do you find yourself using these words daily?**

I'm worried that...
I'm afraid that...
I fear that...
And the worst culprit, a case of the "what ifs."

*What if...*
You can easily fill in the blanks.

What if I... have a panic attack in public, at work, or on the plane, and I need to be institutionalized?

What if the... plane crashes, my kids get killed in a car crash, or if my kids are kidnapped?

What if I... lose my job, what if, what if, what if... ?

The worry, the fear, the "what if's" are never-ending, insatiable beasts!

Stop fanning the flames of your anxiety!

Cut your fears off at the root! Choke them and starve them. It is important to begin feeding the right words and feelings into your mind.

***Is it really this simple?*** Yes!

Instead of saying the word "worried," change it to "concerned." What a difference that will make to your brain!

Begin now. Make that a part of your vocabulary, and lose the word "worried"... it is useless! It does not make you sound more caring to those around you, and it does not take away guilt. It simply does nothing for you.

### Write a Good Mind Script
Your mind does not know the difference between an actual event and your imagination's conjuring up of a frightening or anxiety-

producing event. So, mentally replace a negative scenario with a good script. You are the master of your own mind – create happy endings, expect the best to happen.

*Fear is excitement without the breath.*

**Fritz Perls, M.D**

# CHAPTER II

# Role of Hypnosis

*Our deepest fear is not that we are inadequate.
Our deepest fear is that we are powerful beyond
measure.*

**Marianne Williamson**

## Role of Hypnosis

When your mind is relaxed, it can accept positive input, as long as you support it with actions as well. Let me set the record straight here: Only you can control your mind! Hypnosis is not someone swinging a watch in front of your face and making you do something against your will. This idea is simply not accurate. True therapeutic hypnosis can help many issues; unfortunately, people rule it out because of preconceived ideas stemming from those things that the media shows simply for shock value. Please don't confuse "stage hypnosis" with clinical hypnotherapy. Being called on stage to do a variety of crazy things is equivalent to a Las Vegas act, it is not therapeutic hypnosis.

I strongly suggest that you find a reputable hypnotherapist in your area and try a few sessions. You can easily do self-hypnosis once you've been through a session or two. Ask your therapist to show you how you can achieve this deep, relaxed state in your own home, and then do it! I find that many people are given wonderful tools, but once home, they never open the box!

**Why does it work?**

"Hypnosis works by bypassing the critical conscious mind (usually through relaxation or linguistic techniques), and speaking directly to the unconscious in a language which it understands – pattern, association and metaphor. The unconscious mind is basically in charge."

*abouthypnosis.com; Stephen Walkin, Ph.D.*

## Don't be an "Alice"

A woman named Alice came to me for hypnosis sessions, hoping to rid herself of fearful thoughts. After several sessions, it became very clear that Alice loved to relive her panic attacks. I advised her to stop recycling these negative stories. But, time after time, she repeated her negative experiences to me and to anyone else who would listen. When you constantly repeat or retell negative experiences, your mind does not know the difference between what happened in the past or what is happening now! Your mind and body experience the same stress every time the event is relived, as you think or talk about it. For example, when Alice retold what the event felt like, how she couldn't breathe and would never be able to be in that store or elevator again, she would begin, once again, to experience her heart racing, hands getting sweaty, and all of the other common and uncomfortable feelings that go along with anxiety. She wore her anxious thoughts like a badge of honor. Alice was wasting my time and her money – she did not want to get better. She liked the attention she was receiving from her family and friends, and she kept her fears very alive. Don't become an "Alice."

## Trouble-Talkers Beware!

Should you talk about your feelings? Absolutely! Incessantly? No!

I feel that you only need to tell your particular experience three times, to three different people, and be done with it. Otherwise, your mind will thrive on it. You must starve those thoughts out of your mind! You can tell your confidants, whether it be your spouse, a best friend, your doctor, or your therapist, which may mean a counselor or a member of the clergy. After that, your retelling of a particular negative experience begins feeding your brain, and your brain will think it's OK for this to keep happening. In fact, your mind will begin to perpetuate the cycle, and it will actually help the anxiety to occur more often!

This principle is true. I've lived it and have met hundreds, if not thousands, of people who have experienced this cycle, and I can unequivocally tell you – stop feeding your anxiety by reliving it over and over again! Your mind and body will begin accepting this as your way of living and will give you more of it!

This means...

When you stop the negative chatter, you begin choking off the anxiety. Did you know that you can create an anxiety attack just by thinking about a certain situation? And the reverse is true. When you think about positive thoughts and outcomes, you retrain your brain to like and accept the thoughts that make you feel great. Your mind and body will go along with this and will send out calming hormones, instead of the old "flight or fight" response. When you are focusing on negative or fearful thoughts, your brain and body respond as if you're in real danger.

Dr. Claire Weeks, the author of *Hope and Help for Your Nerves*, said that once you start having panic attacks, your mind becomes like a well-oiled trigger on a gun and just keeps firing off. Don't oil your "trigger." Starve it, dry it out, and those anxious thoughts will shrivel up and die!

*The components of anxiety, stress, fear, and anger do not exist independently of you in the world. They simply do not exist in the physical world, even though we talk about them as if they do.*

**Dr. Wayne Dyer**

## Plants & Me?

Take two potted plants and keep them in your house. Water one as needed, and take some time to move it into the light, or dust off the leaves, and just give it a bit of TLC every day.

Don't water the other plant or do anything with it, simply ignore it. After a week or two, evaluate each plant. What would you expect to happen to each plant? This is the simplest visual I can use to show you that you're not that much different from those plants.

Whatever you feed and care for will live, thrive, and blossom, and whatever you ignore will starve, shrivel up and die. Now apply this principle to your thinking. First, stop watering and fertilizing your mind with words of fear.

Begin right now to face those fears that are not based in reality but have haunted you like some "bump in night" – nothing more than a branch hitting your window.

Which potted plant do you know you can be?

See it, believe it, and you won't be able to stop it from happening.

Your thoughts are that powerful!

*Flowers grow out of darker moments*

**Corita Kent**

# CHAPTER III

# Talk Is Cheap

*The game of life is a game of boomerangs. Our thoughts, deeds, and words return to us sooner or later with astounding accuracy.*

**Florence Scovel Shinn**

## Talk is Cheap

By introducing new words into your life, you will begin to strangle those old anxious fears. Here's a new list of words that I suggest you begin using now:

Instead of saying, "I'm so worried" – change the word worry to *concerned*.

If you tend to say "It's too hard for me to change" or "It's too hard for...," then change "hard" to *"challenge."* Begin saying: "This is a challenge that I will get through." Life can be "challenging" – don't use words like difficult, hard, stressful, painful, etc.

I'm sure you've heard this one before – but now apply it! Change the "I can't" to... *"I can."*

For example, say:

"I can accomplish this."

"I can walk into that store or onto that plane, and nothing will happen to me."

"This is a challenge, but I can do it."

This one is my favorite.  Learn to say "So What!" – a lot.

Saying this can be very powerful. If you're panicked about going out or driving a car, whatever your particular fears are, just say to yourself, "So what if I feel scared, so what! I've been through this before. Big deal. So what!" You may not believe it. In fact, you probably won't believe what you're saying. Say it anyway! Keep saying it, and you will find that your mind will accept it. Often, it is as simple as that. We tend to make life difficult for ourselves, don't we? How's that been working for you? Stop analyzing and start doing!

ooooo

*The only thing we have to fear is fear itself.*

**Franklin D. Roosevelt**

*Change your thoughts and you change your world.*

**Norman Vincent Peale**

*Do not go where the path may lead, go instead where there is no path and leave a trail.*

**Ralph Waldo Emerson**

# CHAPTER IV

# 10 Easy Steps to Peace

*Peace I leave with you, my peace I give unto you: not as the world giveth, give I unto you. Let not your heart be troubled, neither let it be afraid.*

**Jesus, John 14:27**

## Ten Easy Steps to Peace

*Follow this advice. Read it over and over again. Keep it by your bedside, and read a passage or a quote first thing in the morning and last thing at night.*

*The road to peace is easy – once you welcome it. I've walked the difficult path for many years, with debilitating fears, and I can now help guide you toward the path of peace, joy, and true inner happiness that no situation can take away from you. You will be your own safety zone, your own shelter from the storms of life, because you'll know that like any storm, they pass. Things do get better, the sky becomes bright again, and you'll appreciate it even more. No storm, no awful situation, stays forever. You will pass through it and be even stronger for it.*

*The following ten steps may seem almost too easy, but follow them anyway. Stop analyzing. Stop thinking that your case is the worst – it is not.*

*Many others have walked that difficult road. This is your blueprint for an easier one.*

*Be not afraid of life. Believe that life is worth living, and your belief will help create the fact.*

**Henry James**

*If I had to limit my advice on healthier living to just one tip, it would be simply to learn how to breathe correctly.*

**Andrew Weil, M.D.**

# #1 - The Art of Breathing

I know you've read and been told many times to "take a deep breath" and all will be well, and it is that easy...well, almost. Here's a quick trick: imagine a baby's chubby little belly rising up and down as he lies on his back, with just a diaper on. A baby knows how to breathe correctly, and so did you at one time. It's the way we're designed to breathe. You just forgot how to do it along the road of life. Keep the image of the relaxed breathing of a baby in your mind.

Now, relax your stomach muscles as if you were that baby or a Raggedy Ann Doll, limp and loose all over. Take in a breath through your nose, keeping your mouth closed. When you see and feel your stomach rising, slowly exhale through your nose again. Practice keeping your mouth closed, using only your nostrils to breathe in and out. When you do this, your brain automatically registers that there's nothing to fear; therefore, no adrenaline is pumped through your body in preparation for a "fight or flight" reaction.

You see, your body does not know the difference between actual fear and imagined fear; it's all one and the same for it. If you breathe rapidly, with your mouth opened, pulling in air as if hyperventilating, your brain registers that something is wrong... and that you'd better get out of there! When you start relaxing your breath, by closing your mouth and breathing more slowly via your nostrils, your brain begins registering that all is well, and voila, no more anxiety-producing adrenaline pumping through your body, and no panic attack!

## The Quick Way to Belly-Breathe Your Way to Peace...

#1  Close your mouth.
#2  Let your body go loose & limp like a Raggedy Ann Doll.
#3  Press on the side of your nose with your index finger and close off one nostril.
#4  Breathe in and out slowly, three times.
#5  Repeat on alternate side.

*Emotional and physical states can be altered by changing the breathing pattern.*

**Wilhelm Reich**

*Everything in life changes you in some way. Even the smallest things. If you do not accept these changes you do not accept yourself. For through these changes brings new and greater things to you, making you wiser, as time progresses. To avoid these changes is a loss. You only live your life once. Do not waste a minute of it avoiding things. Let them come to you, and learn from them. There is always tomorrow.*

**Adam R. Gwizdala**

## #2- Accept and Act

It truly doesn't matter if you feel frightened, unreal, or unsteady. These feelings are nothing more than exaggerated physical and emotional reactions to stress, and, under the circumstances, these feelings are quite normal! Acceptance is your key out of the world of panic. Do not add "what ifs" to your vocabulary. The fear of your fear will keep it alive. Learn to say "so what?" and "big deal" when you feel anxious, and you'll be amazed at just how quickly you can retrain your body to relax.

If your religious or spiritual belief is that you'll be going to a better place after you leave this earth, then truly believe that! Embrace that belief with all of your mind, heart, and soul, knowing that if the worse thing did happen, so what! You'd be in a better place...right? And, if you believe in nothing, that you would just vanish, then, so what! You wouldn't know a thing! Enjoy this life, with all its ups and downs, and stop worrying about every little thing that takes place in your body. Find it interesting, instead. If you change your words from "what's happening to me?" to "this is interesting," your brain will go right along with you.

Even Cary Grant, the most dashing, debonair screen idol the world has known, never felt like "Cary Grant." He had a tough beginning; he was told his mother had died when, actually, she was placed in a mental institution. He left his country, joined a circus, and was not that suave, highly-educated man we see in the dozens of his movies, but, rather, a struggling performer named Archibald Leech. However, once Hollywood discovered that they could make a lot of money on that dashing character, he was soon typecast. He played his role over and over again, till one day...he did indeed become "Cary Grant."

*"I pretended to be somebody I wanted to be until finally I became that person. Or, he became me."*

**Cary Grant**

**Who do you want to be? How do you want to feel?**

Perhaps you have a mentor, someone you'd love to be like; it doesn't matter if you've never met that person or even if they're alive or dead! You may want to conjure up that image, and imagine what they'd do in a fearful situation- how they would react- and, perhaps, you will become the better part of your mentor.

Act the way you want to be, and soon you'll be the way you're acting!!

*Within each of us lies the power of our consent to health and sickness, to riches and poverty, to freedom and to slavery. It is we who control these, and not another.*

**Richard Bach**

## #3 - You are not sick

If you have a clean bill of health from your doctor, other than being told that you need to relax and/or that you need to handle stress better, then don't talk yourself into an illness. Believe what your doctor has told you. Your words are powerful, and they can be used as weapons or healing tonics.

The physical sensations you experience with anxiety don't make you ill. These feelings are just unpleasant, not dangerous. Nothing worse will happen to you!

ooooo

**Expect miracles to happen! Face your fears and they will melt away. Don't give them validity.**

*You can set yourself up to be sick, or you can choose to stay well.*

**Wayne Dyer**

# #4 - It's OK To Feel Anxious

Let your feelings come. They've been in charge for a long time, and you've kept them alive by fearing them. It is important to experience these feelings in a different way. Not only by saying "so what" or "big deal," but by retraining your thoughts to acknowledge these uncomfortable, even horrible, feelings by saying things like "isn't this interesting." Then, notice what your body does once your mind has registered that you are not afraid. It really is interesting. If you can make yourself anxious, then you can also reduce your anxiety. By thinking different thoughts and breathing correctly, you can get yourself out of a panic attack.

I can remember the moment I lost my fear of fear. I was determined to drive alone. I had only been able to drive with someone else in the car, someone who would be able to take over in case I fainted, ran screaming from the car, or, the ultimate... died! The disastrous possibilities I envisioned were endless.

You know how creative you are when imagining what could go wrong. One day, I decided to overcome this fear of driving solo and asked my husband to follow me in his car. Sounds easy,

Wrong. I had the absolute-worst panic attack about a half mile from our home, as I was heading further from the safety of home. There I was in the car, doing everything wrong. I was rapidly pulling air into my lungs, resulting in tingling and numbness in my hands, while worrying about whether I could hold onto the wheel. Would I get into an accident and kill myself? Or, worse yet, hurt other people? I was just about to pull over to abandon the car and jump into my husband's, when a wave of anger engulfed me. I cried out loud, *"Are you willing to become an invalid? Will people forever be carting you around? Will this ever end?"*

I yelled out, *"I'm greater than this fear!"* And, in that moment, I also said, *"Wow, isn't this interesting, look what I did to my body."* Within minutes my hands stopped tingling, and my breath was normal. I eventually waved my husband away and I went solo. I was flying high!

When you are afraid, practice your breathing and even yell out loud something like, "Oh, big deal, this is just another bout of misfired adrenaline." And you win. You get stronger each time and, eventually, you'll know, really know, that whatever happens to you, wherever you are, you can handle it!

*You may encounter many defeats, but you must not be defeated. In fact, it may be necessary to encounter the defeats, so you can know who you are, what you can rise from, how you can still come out of it.*

**Maya Angelou**

# #5 - Your Thoughts Become Your Reality

To illustrate just how amazing our thoughts are, here's a story that was told to me, concerning my paternal grandfather.  He passed away before I was born, but in the family scrapbook I saw a dapper, charming-looking fellow, who looked like he owned the world.  However, I learned that he suffered from asthma, which must have been debilitating without inhalers or anti-inflammatory drugs during his day.  One night, he was having terrible time breathing. He was wheezing and felt like he was suffocating.  All he wanted was to open his bedroom window and take in a breath of fresh air which actually existed back then; but he was too tired to get up and was sure that he would lay there and surely die.  However, his Italian temper rose, and he cursed his asthma and reached for his work boot by the side of his bed.  With all the strength he had, he tossed it at the window.   As he heard the crash of the glass, he quickly felt the rush of the cool, crisp night air and took in a deep breath.   He fell asleep within minutes, thinking he'd clean up the mess in the morning.

When the sun rose, he fumbled for his eyeglasses, not wanting to step on glass from the window, and he was stunned to see that the only window in the room was not broken. How could that be? He looked around the room and saw that he had broken the glass on a small cabinet near the window. Grandfather had not opened a window to the outside, he had opened a window in his mind to the power of his thoughts. Think about it. The sound of broken glass convinced his brain that the window was open and fresh air was rushing in. His brain had recreated the feeling and scent of the night air, which had relaxed him enough that his wheezing stopped, and he was able to sleep.

**What the mind believes, you will conceive.**

*The thing you fear most has no power. Your fear of it is what has the power. Facing the truth really will set you free.*

**Oprah Winfrey**

## #6 - Stay in the Present

We've all been told to "live in the moment," but it is important to focus on this phrase and learn what it truly means. If you understand how this concept works, you'll be able to apply it. "Live in the moment" is said so often that it's just something we say, like "Hello, how are you?"

Not staying in the present means that you are dealing with classic anticipatory fear and that you're living in the unrealistic future. For example, you're afraid of entering an elevator for fear it might get stuck, and then you begin to worry about feeling claustrophobic. You are concerned that you might feel dizzy, faint, or start screaming "let me out of here!" should the doors open up too slowly, and then, the men in the "white coats" will surely come for you!

Your mind conjures up all of these fearful thoughts, even before you press the elevator button. The problem is that your mind does not know if this event is really happening or if you're just thinking that it may happen. On a cellular level, when you go through these future catastrophic thoughts, you put your body through a lot of stress.

Staying in the present means just that- staying in the moment. Let's use the same elevator scenario, which you can change to a plane, car, or whatever you fear most. Look at where you're standing. Are you really trapped? No. Glide your hand over the elevator button and really look at it. Nice metal. Notice it. Are you stuck? No. By focusing on what is happening right now, you can train your mind not to race forward. Notice the numbers in the elevator as they light up for each floor. Think of this as an interesting event. Marvel at how the lights pop up for each floor. Wonder how that happens. Stay in the moment. Notice a person standing near you. Observe the colors and the sounds, and be glad that you're alive and that you can feel and see. By diverting and focusing your mind on things other than your fears, before you know it, the experience is over. This stops the thoughts, the cycle of "what ifs."

Should you run into a bout of "what ifs," try this: "What if I enjoy my life? "What if I can handle everything that life sends my way?" Haven't you been doing that all along anyway?

*I believe in God, only I spell it Nature.*

**Frank Lloyd Wright**

# #7 - What, me worry?

Did you know that over 90% of what we worry about never actually happens?

That's a fact. Therefore, it is very unrealistic to worry. But now that you know this, how do you stop? Just like everything else, you just begin. You start to train yourself not to worry, and that happens very quickly as you become aware of your words.

Changing your words has the power to change everything.

Instead of saying "What am I going to do?" start saying, "I can handle it." You have already handled many situations, possibly better than you thought you would. So don't throw yourself into a tailspin, with a bunch of "what if's" and "oh, no's." Say to yourself, "I can do this." When you say this, your body will immediately relax. There is no added rush of adrenalin, no headache, no hyperventilating, just a calm feeling that you will handle the situation.

Perhaps you find yourself using phrases such as "this is awful," "what a mess we're in," or "what a disaster." These catastrophic words and thoughts will only inhibit you from dealing with situations in a calm and rational manner.

Train yourself now. Learn to say something as simple as.... "This is interesting, and I'll handle it." You'll be amazed at the results, and you will handle it without all the drama. Remember, you cannot hold two strong emotions at the same time. One always wins out.

Let your emotions be positive ones. Consciously focus on being at peace. Don't become anxious about something that may never take place.

*Happy is the man who has broken the chains which hurt the mind, and has given up worrying once and for all.*

**Ovid**

*A person knowing the power of the word, becomes very careful of his conversation. He has only to watch the reaction of his words to know that the words do not return void. Through his spoken word, man is continually making laws for himself.*

**Florence Scovel Shinn**

# #8 - Your Words are Magic!

Did you ever wish you had a magic wand to make all your fears, panic attacks, and uncomfortable feelings just go away? Of course you have! Life doesn't hand us magic wands, but it does supply us with the power to change our reactions, and that begins and ends with the words we use. You have probably heard it all before – "As a man thinks, so shall he be," and on and on. But stop, learn, and listen. It's true!

This principle is so important that it must become a part of you: When you change your words and your thoughts, you change everything. Try this test: Every morning, when you get up, conscientiously repeat to yourself, "Life is good and I feel great." Now, you may not feel this is true at all, but say it anyway. Say it three times. Say it every morning for three weeks.

As you say that phrase, you can add extra power to it by imagining yourself truly feeling that way. See yourself with a smile on your face. Imagine how your life would be if you did feel that way. What would you be doing? What would you like to be doing in order to feel that your life is good and that you feel great?

This should take only a minute or two each morning.

At the end of the three weeks...stop! On the morning that you stop saying the phrase, notice how your mind wants you to say it. You may feel that something is missing.

While you have probably never said those words every morning in your life, in just three weeks your very being has become attached to the words and wants you to continue repeating them.

Take note of how you feel. Did you feel better, stronger, or happier during that time? Did you miss saying your phrase? Remember, what you say and what you focus upon, whether good or bad, will become your reality. It's just the way it works.

If the phrase is not one you're comfortable with, choose one that resonates with you. Make it simple, positive, believable, and present-tense. An unbelievable statement would be, "I'm Oprah and I love my work." A believable thought for her, but not for you!

You want to be realistic, but you also need to aim high. You want the saying to become a part of you, even though you may be feeling far from it now. Train yourself to accept positive thinking, about who you are and about how you respond to life.

**Examples of what you can say:**

*I attract health and wealth into my life.*

*My body is strong, and I'm fearless.*

*I'm peaceful and protected.*

*I have nothing to fear, and I enjoy my life.*

Choose one of these sayings, or create one for yourself. Stay true to that one saying for the entire three weeks. You can change your sayings, but each time you do make a change, stay with it for a full three week period.

*True happiness is... to enjoy the present, without anxious dependence on the future.*

**Lucius Annaeus Seneca**

*A cheerful frame of mind, reinforced by relaxation... is the medicine that puts all ghosts of fear on the run.*

**George Matthew Adams**

## #9 - Believe and Enjoy!

I believe that we are divine beings who come from a creator who is good. Our source is one of peace, love, harmony, and well-being. Therefore, when we are out of balance, we are out of alignment with all of those good qualities which we are meant to possess. In other words, we fell off our track in life! And when we put ourselves back on-track, how sweet it is!

We are then lined up, linked up to the power, the power of God.

Whether you pray, meditate, do yoga, sit by the ocean, or rest at a park- wherever you feel calm, connect to your higher power. Don't get caught up in the history of it. Don't analyze things to death – just experience it! Then trust. Trust that God, the Universe, or whatever you call it, is working for you, not against you. Just that simple thought can lift burdens of worry off your mind and begin to calm you immediately.

Your life is unfolding just the way it should. Accept it and go forward.

Starving Your Fears

○ ○ ○ ○ ○

*You block your dream when you allow your fear
to grow bigger than your faith.*

**Mary Manin Morrissey**

*You are never too old to set another goal or to dream a new dream.*

**C.S. Lewis**

# #10 - Do it scared!

One day, I was in my dugout of fear, sequestered away in my apartment. I was afraid that I would never be able to take care of my family. I was newly divorced, my sons were young, and I needed a job. Trying to face these realities, while coping with debilitating fears, was beyond overwhelming. At that time, phrases like "stress management" weren't even used, but words like 'crazy' and 'insane' were.

It was sink or swim time. My money was almost gone, and I needed a miracle. My miracle came in the form of a friend, who said to me, "You're experiencing the fear, the panic attacks, right here in your apartment, so why not go out and find that job? The worst thing that could happen to you is that you'll feel the way you're feeling now, only you'll be making progress."

Ding, ding, ding! Yes! Still difficult to do when you're so afraid to venture outside, but it made sense to me.

As much as I hated it at first, I left my apartment and looked for a job, even while filled with fear. Why not? I've been doing most things afraid anyway, so what's the big deal about this, I asked myself. As I changed my thinking, I began moving towards the possibility that I could do this.

What is the difference between sitting at home with all the worrisome thoughts, eventually leading to anxiety attacks, or going out and risking having them in public? Not much, except that someone might notice you breathing into a brown paper bag because you're hyper-ventilating. And who cares if they do? I did that many times, and guess what? No one cared! Many anxious people tend to hyperventilate (over-breathing) and breathing into a bag is to "re-breathe" your exhaled carbon dioxide ($CO_2$) in the hopes of bringing your body back to a normal pH level. I was once so comforted knowing that I had my paper bag with me that my breathing immediately calmed down; however, when I returned home... there it sat on my bed. Mind over matter!

The bottom line is that you will not only feel better about yourself once you've accomplished something, but you'll exercise those muscles of trust, faith, and fearlessness.

Do it scared! And after a short time, you'll just be doing it, and it will no longer be a big deal at all.

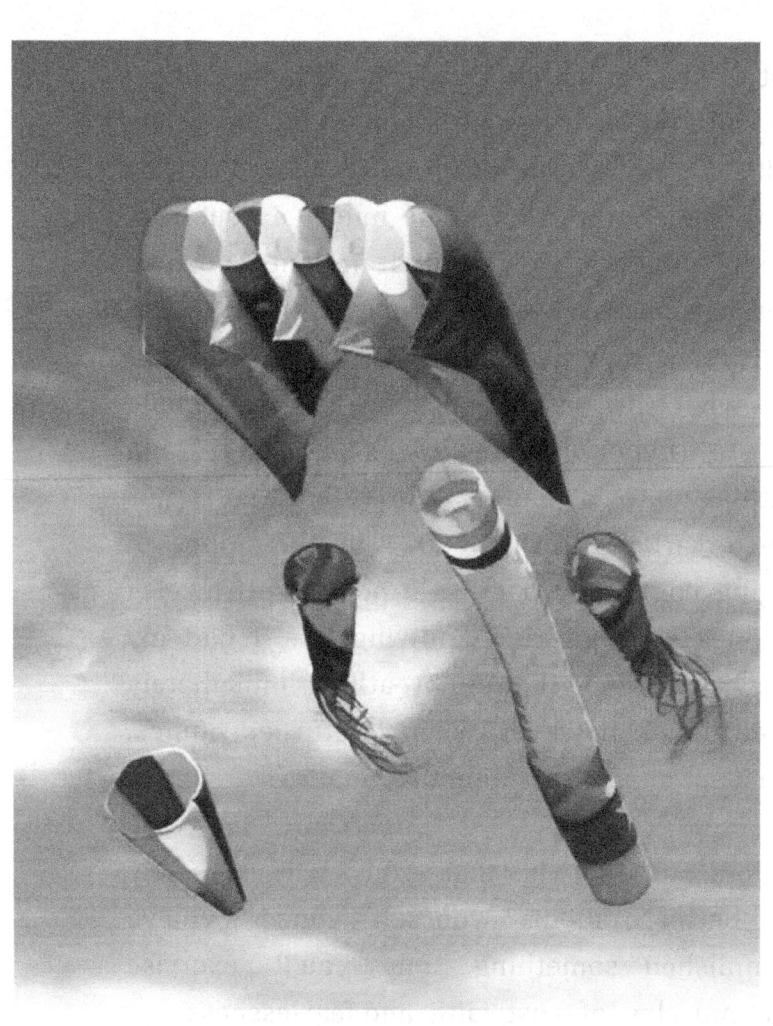

*Hope is knowing that people, like kites, are made to be lifted up.*

**Anonymous**

The following are true stories, from the marvelous people I've met while in private practice. Only their names have been changed.

I hope you will find them as inspiring as I did, while working along with them. Everyone we meet is our teacher, and I have learned much by paying attention to the lessons I must learn in order to pass along the knowledge I have gained.

*There is no such thing in anyone's life as an unimportant day.*

**Alexander Woollcott**

# CHAPTER V

# Janeen's Story

## Janeen's Story

She walked into my office like a fire was licking at her heels. She was not shy or frightened that day, she was angry.

Janeen whisked in with her blonde hair bouncing in her own breeze, and even before pleasantries were spoken, she asked, "What the hell is wrong with me?" I laughed out loud. She took me by surprise, and I immediately knew that I was going to love working with her.

I quickly found out that she did not have a history of panic attacks and was not, typically, an anxious person. But, suddenly, she couldn't function in stores and was avoiding shopping, which she had adored to the point of being obsessive about it. She said that shopping was her guilty pleasure.

She stared at me with her piercing blue eyes and wanted an answer to what was happening to her...now! She wanted to get on with her life, to go shopping again without thinking about it, and to get rid of this "monster," as she called it.

## Nightmare in Nordstrom's

Janeen adored shopping; it was her favorite hobby. She was always looking for something new to take home, especially something that satisfied her passion for shoes and purses. Since she was single, with a full time job, she was free to shop on Saturdays, by herself or with a friend.

Janeen's first brush with panic occurred while shopping in one of her favorite stores, Nordstrom's. It was a typical Saturday afternoon. She was alone and flipping through the sales racks, hunting for new shoes. Janeen said she began to feel uncomfortably warm and a little light-headed. She took off her sweater and continued to shop, although the lights seemed brighter, and, suddenly, she began to feel trapped. She had no idea why but, quite uncharacteristically, she just wanted to leave and forget about shopping. She walked quickly to the cashier, clutching the few items she already had, wanting desperately to get out of there.

When she got to the counter, the woman ahead of her had a problem with her credit card. As she waited in line, Janeen's heart began to race, and she broke out in a cold sweat. She had no idea what was happening. She didn't feel ill, just very scared. As she pressed the few articles of clothing and a pretty pink purse to her chest, her thoughts ran wild. Should she bolt out of there, leaving her treasures behind? Was she going to faint? Die? Throw up? The more her thoughts raced, the more frightened she became, and just when she thought "I'm getting out of here" – the cashier asked for the next person in line.

For a moment, Janeen's mind began to calm, as she focused on setting the articles down, getting her credit card out, and trying to smile as if nothing was wrong. Everything seemed to be calming down inside of her, but soon her anxiety level shot up, and this time it was worse. Just as she put away her card, while thinking that she could quickly escape into the outside air, the cashier asked for her card back. The store was having trouble processing some credit cards, and the cashier explained that she had to manually enter the numbers. Janeen's heart was racing, and her knees were so weak she didn't know what to do. She managed to sign the credit card slip with a very shaky hand and then grabbed her bag, bolting toward the exit... when the security alarm went off as she walked out the door. She heard a woman calling, "Miss, miss!" and she turned to see two women coming towards her. They assured her that it was probably their fault, but she would need to empty her bag out.

At this point, Janeen felt that she might have a stroke, or something worse, because her body was enduring so much stress. She knew she must look guilty too, with her eyes darting about, looking for a way to get outside for some air. She tried to make light of the situation, but she was frozen with fear. They went through her bag twice as each time she exited the alarm went off – this was unbelievable! Had it been any other day, she would have laughed this off and joked with the women, but today was not that day. At her third attempt to leave, with the alarm still buzzing away, one woman asked to have her take the new pink purse and swing it by the alarm. As she did so, it sounded the alarm and the culprit was found.

Tucked inside a zippered area was that big, plastic, white tag, sending off sound waves and escalating Janeen's own wave of terror!

By the time she got to her car, she was exhausted. She sat there for a while, gathering her strength, sipping on the remnants of what was now a cold cup of coffee; it had been sitting in the car for nearly two hours. Her head was pounding with pain as she took some Tylenol that she found at the bottom of her purse. When she felt calm enough, she drove home, and her life was forever changed.

Janeen went to her doctor and all health concerns were ruled out. She was in perfect health, and her doctor assured her that this was probably an isolated incident. Perhaps it was due to her not eating breakfast, too little sleep, or too much caffeine, and he told her to just go on with her life. However, this experience left Janeen feeling helpless and very afraid. The intensity of the first panic attack can be compared to a nine on the Richter's scale of earthquakes to the body. There can be aftershocks of fear, which may come again and again, while there's nothing to do but wait for them to come. I understood Janeen all too well, having gone through this myself. Other people often don't understand panic and anxiety, and this journey can be very lonely at times. One intense panic attack can truly change your life – and I needed to show Janeen that it would change it for the better. She was about to learn how to cope with, and know that she could handle, any situation in life.

Janeen stopped shopping for about two months because she had frightened herself into a mild depression. Now she was beginning to have anxious thoughts while grocery shopping, and since she lived alone, with no family nearby, she knew she needed help. She had gotten my name through someone at work, and she was now ready to begin finding her way back into life.

## It's Shoe-Time!

Janeen was angry, she'd had enough, and that was good. You can't hold two strong emotions at the same time, one will win out. In this case, Janeen's anger propelled her to come see me.

I don't think that it is necessary to determine what causes an anxiety attack (after ruling out any physical causes), because, even if the source is pinpointed, you still must teach your mind and body how to relax, to learn to breathe correctly, and to practice these skills daily via meditation/self-hypnosis. Janeen felt that there was nothing in her life that could have caused this. No childhood traumas or dramas. I didn't probe too deeply. My job was to get her out and about and enjoying life again.

Once that panic attack happened, Janeen began to set herself up for failure every day. She so feared having one, she obsessed about it every waking moment. She fed and fed that fear so much that it was now insatiable, and it was thriving on all of her negative thoughts, growing ever larger and more dominant.

Janeen was very open to hypnosis, so we began her sessions with it from day one. She had heard of others being helped by this process, therefore, she was already receptive for this method to work. Hypnosis is a wonderful way to quickly relax the body and mind, by using the creative power of the mind to visualize how situations can change, just by changing a thought. Janeen could easily visualize how the situation in Nordstrom's could have been different if she had not fed her fears. She visualized herself in the store and could feel her skin becoming warmer, just as it had at the very beginning of her panic attack.

Only this time, in her mind, she took off her sweater, took a few deep, relaxing diaphragmatic breaths (belly breaths), and focused on how much fun she was having. She told herself that no matter what happened, she could handle it. During her session, I also reinforced that, even though the worst panic attack had flooded over her, she still did handle it. She paid for her items, she endured the alarms going off, and she had made it home safely. This technique helped her to practice exactly what to do to immediately lower her anxiety. By refocusing her thinking, she could halt the adrenalin rush and the feelings of panic.

Janeen came to my office faithfully twice a week for two weeks, for hypnosis and visualization sessions, and was also meditating two to three minutes per day at home. And, as any good "flight instructor" knows, there comes a time when the student must fly the plane alone. It was time for Janeen to take flight. When I first told her that her assignment for the following session would be to go back to Nordstrom's and buy something, using her new-found tools, she jerked her head around as if to say "No way!" and then took a deep, belly breath, relaxed her shoulders, and looked squarely at me and said, "Done."

A few days later, Janeen walked into my office, beaming, and stuck her foot out for me to see her new pink and black sandals and her new skirt. She looked happy and relaxed and was extremely proud of herself. She admitted that she had needed to use all of the "tools" she had learned while in the store, and that she did it easily, without feeding the old fears.

The scary and uncomfortable feelings did start to rise up inside as she walked into the store, but she had handled it! Janeen said she began to feel warm and dizzy, and for a few seconds she thought "Here we go again," and she thought about running out. But, she said her mind immediately conjured up her visualization sessions. She could hear me saying, "Do not feed the fear," and like second nature, she put her body into a relaxed state quickly, by using diaphragmatic breathing and consciously relaxing her body until it was loose and limp. As she did this, she felt her anxiety level drop almost immediately, from a level eight (10 being the highest) to one. She thought about being stronger than those empty fears, and she reminded herself that she could handle anything. She realized that she was through the worst of it and now knew how to look that fear in the eyes and starve it, by cutting off the negative thoughts.

For Janeen, it was like learning how to ride a bike. Now that she knows what to do, she will never forget how to respond, regardless of the circumstances.

Janeen is back to shopping regularly and, recently, did lot of shopping for her wedding. She said that it was ironic that she had to shop for items for her bridesmaids, family, friends, and fiancé. She wondered if the first panic attack had been a blessing in disguise, because a panic attack during the stress of planning a wedding could have altered the course of her marriage plans. She'll never know, but she is now confident that she can thwart her fears, by practicing positive visualizations (just a few minutes) every day and by breathing deeply when stressed.

*The purpose of life is to live it, to taste experience to the utmost, to reach out eagerly and without fear for newer and richer experience.*

**Eleanor Roosevelt**

*Change your thoughts and you change your world.*

**Norman Vincent Peale**

# CHAPTER VI

# Kenny's Story

## Kenny's Story

One of my colleagues, Susan, was having a difficult time in her therapy sessions with Kenny. A single father in his early 30's, Kenny was hit hard with panic attacks. Susan had been treating him for almost a year and felt that they were not making progress. Kenny seemed to take five steps forward and then eight steps backwards. It was as frustrating to him as it was to her. He was only able to drive the few short blocks to Susan's office, which was very difficult for him.

Kenny's panic attacks were so intense that he was unable to work, and he was forced to live with his sister. He was able to collect disability, due to his inability to work. But, this provided barely enough money to make ends meet, which only added to his stress and exacerbated his anxiety attacks. Even though my schedule was quite full, I did agree to go to his home to meet with him, as he could not make the drive to my office.

## Kenny's Story

I met Kenny on a warm, bright June day. As I walked up to the front door, a man's voice called out, requesting that I come to the back yard. I went through the back gate and was almost blinded by the shimmering sunlight bouncing off of the water from the swimming pool. Kenny was sitting at a small table, with an umbrella shading him. He slowly stood up and offered me a very nervous handshake; his eyes were lowered, and he politely asked if I wanted a soda. I could feel his apprehension, and that he had quite possibly given up hope. I was just one more person he would have to explain his situation to, and he would still be stuck – stuck in his sister's house and trapped within his own prison.

He was a tall, lean man with green, tired-looking eyes. Even though he was in his early 30's, he appeared older, due to the way his shoulders drooped from the fatigue that settled over his body. He lit his second cigarette, of the ten minutes I was there, and barely said a word.

After working with Susan for nearly a year and a few other therapists before her, I could understand his suspicion of me – and the tiredness of having to explain his story all over again. I know – because I've been there too.

I asked about his little girl, Jenny, who was 7 years old. He told me that his panic attacks began after his wife had left him, when Jenny was only a baby. Kenny was caught completely off guard by her departure, and he'd had to face the overwhelming fact that he was left alone to raise Jenny. While puffing on yet another cigarette, he told me that he had small bouts of anxiety during the past five years, but the blasts of panic had grown larger, scarier, and more debilitating over the past two years. The more he felt that he *had* to overcome it, that he *had* to take care of Jenny, that he *had* to keep his job – the worse the panic became. The pressure he was adding to himself had taken its toll, and the thing he feared the most had happened. He had no job, was living with his sister, and felt that he had let his daughter down.

The poolside welcome didn't fool me. For a man sitting outside, he looked pasty white. He probably spent very little time lounging by the pool. I think that he greeted me outside because he didn't want to invite me into his home, into his life. He was an angry, sad man who was sinking quickly.

Kenny had been on several different antidepressants over the past two years, but he didn't like the side-effects and had stopped taking them.

Kenny confessed that he had begun drinking a beer or two each night, just so he could get to sleep without waking up in a cold sweat, caused by a nighttime panic attack.

My heart ached for this young man. I knew that, at one time, he felt on top of the world. That his body had been strong, and he had great hopes of having his own business and building a home for his family, and now, those dreams were gone, and, worse yet, so was his hope.

## What To Do?

We sat by the pool for over two hours. I told him my story, and, at that point, he became more interested in what I had to say. I was the first therapist he had met who had actually experienced what he was going through. In fact, I was the first person he had spoken with that could share his feelings. For the first time, he looked me straight in the eyes and I saw that undeniable glimmer of hope. This was a start – his journey to wellness was about to begin!

## The Plan

"Kenny, what if I told you that you'll never be the person you were before, but you can be even better. Would you believe me?" He just stared at me with a quizzical look.

I explained that, perhaps, he was trying so desperately to get back to what his life was like before his wife left that he was adding layers and layers of stress, resulting in horrible panic attacks. He was really listening now.

We worked out a schedule for the following month. I would go to his place every Wednesday from noon – 1 p.m., while his sister was at work and Jenny in school. We agreed to do this for four sessions, and, during that time, we would work on getting him to drive to and from my office.

Kenny had been "feeding" his anxiety attacks for a long time, by staying in the past with unforgiveness and hanging on to anger, regret, and loneliness. I knew this would be a difficult leap of faith for him, to trust me and to trust himself.

During the first two sessions, I took Kenny through a relaxation/visualization process. It's also called hypnotherapy, though I rarely use that term with people who are very anxious because it can frighten them. My hypnotherapy sessions are comprised of creating deep relaxation for the mind/body, while positive messages and a guided visualization is given and accepted by the client. I am not talking about "stage hypnosis," where a bunch of people are told to do strange things, and the crowd goes along with it to get a good belly laugh. This is a clinical process that allows the brain to calm down, in order to see things as they really are. It is positive thinking at a deep level.

Proper breathing was key for Kenny; the only time I saw him inhale deeply was while smoking cigarettes. We first practiced diaphragmatic breathing. (See chapter 4).

While Kenney sat in a comfortable, big, brown chair in the living room, I told him to imagine a beautiful golden light coming down from the heavens just for him. He was to focus on the light, as it moved across and through his body. In doing so, he would feel very relaxed, like a Raggedy Andy doll, while allowing his body to feel comfortably warm. For the first time, I saw his body relax. His shoulders were drooped, his arms and hands not moving. There was no clenched fist or jaw – it was a beautiful sight.

During the first two sessions, I had Kenny imagine that he was smiling and driving. He visualized driving through towns, over bridges, and on long stretches of highway. I kept him in the present, while reinforcing that he was doing this now, today. I asked him to notice how people were allowing him to change lanes, how safe the bridge looked, and how it had stood for many, many years. I told him the world was for him, not against him. He had never thought of that before, and it made quite an impression on him. "The world wants me to succeed, it is not against me," he repeated. The more relaxed, happy, and joyous he felt on our flights of fancy, the more he looked forward to actually doing it and getting on with his life.

By my last visit with Kenny at his home, he had mastered the ability to visualize and, while he looked forward to his visit to my office the following week, there was apprehension in his voice. He was going to drive to see me.

When people leave their "safe space," they often feel apprehensive. But, it's no different than the feelings many people experience when starting a new job, buying a house, or any other major change. The only difference is that people who are prone to anxiety attacks become afraid of the uncomfortable feeling. This makes them even more anxious, resulting in too much adrenaline pumping through their bodies... and bingo! A full blown, terribly-uncomfortable panic attack erupts. When Kenny fully understands that the only way to get over his panic attacks is to go through them, without giving them much notice, he will begin to get well. He must starve the fears at their roots. What you don't feed cannot thrive. It's as simple as that.

After four visits, Kenny had his "tool bag" and was ready to go. He knew how to breathe diaphragmatically, which automatically lessens the panicky feeling and can even stop it cold. He knew how to stay in the present, to not go into the world of "what if's," the useless thoughts that feed the fire of anxiety. He knew that he was in control, even more than he believed. He was aware that he had the power to change his thoughts, and that he needed to dwell on what was good and positive around him. For example, he could focus on his car being in good shape, that his tires were good, and that people are for him, not against him. He understood that everyone suffers and has feelings of being alone, but we are not alone. He knew to be thankful for the roof over his head, no matter whose roof it was, for the fact that he had a lovely, healthy daughter who adored him, and that he could walk, talk, see, and hear. It was time for him to dwell on these things and to let go of what he had no control over- his past.

## The Drive to Forever

At noon on the fifth Wednesday, a warm, sunny July day – Kenny walked into my office. Hurray! We hug. We cry. He smiles, and I can tell that he's on his way to a much better life. He looks stronger; he looks confident.

He did it! He told me that he was uncomfortable at times, but he kept reminding himself to stay in the present. When he first got into the car and began to feel his hands sweat and heart racing a bit, he took a long deep breath, several times, and He touched the inside roof of his car and said a silent "Thank you," reminding himself how lucky he was to have a car, to have a roof over his head.  He kissed a photo of his daughter at a stop light and said, "Thank you."  He reminded himself that it was okay not to feel okay in doing something new.  He reminded himself to change his words.  Instead of saying "This is scary," he said "This is exciting," and he reminded himself that all of this was part of *his* life... no one else's.

I saw Kenny each week for about four months after that, and he had come a long way from the sad man I saw sitting by the pool!  Kenny surrounded his world with positive audio books, and began doing a meditation/prayer every day... only for 5 minutes every morning, but those 5 minutes were empowering ones! He was resetting his mind each day to believe, and know, that he could handle anything that came along.  That life gives all of us challenges, and by changing his thoughts, he would change everything!  He was reprogramming that powerful computer, his mind, and filling it with strong, positive hardware!

In the past, when Kenny was seeing different therapists, talking about his wife leaving and retelling his story over and over again, he was reliving the same anger and panic. His mind and body did not know the difference between what had happened years ago and what was happening now. His mind had become highly sensitized to the trauma he went through, and kept going through, resulting in drenching panic attacks. It is absolutely fine to talk about your feelings, as it's very therapeutic, very healing, but I do question why this has to go on for years. What you talk about is kept alive and thriving – why keep fears alive? Why keep horrible memories so alive? What you should keep alive are thoughts of what is happening now. How you can improve your life. Thankful thoughts. Starve off the negative ones!

It has now been over 3 years since I first met Kenny, and we occasionally bump into each other in stores and exchange Christmas cards. Kenny has a whole new life now. He took a computer course at a local technical school at night and, after 10 months of training, he secured a job in a bank. He and Jenny live in a lovely condo that he was able to purchase with no money down, as he picked up a foreclosure that came through his bank.   Last we spoke, he was dating a woman he met at the church he attends.  And, best of all, he stopped smoking!

*It isn't what you have or who you are or where you are or what you are doing that makes you happy or unhappy. It is what you think about it.*

**Dale Carnegie**

*Whatever the mind of man can conceive and believe, it can achieve.*

**Napoleon Hill**

# CHAPTER VII

# Allison's Story

## Allison's Story

Allison worked in a high-rise filled with attorneys and financial companies. She was the Human Resource manager of a highly successful law firm, where she was extraordinarily busy and stressed. She was married, had a teenage son, and was working to keep her family financially afloat. Her husband had lost his job due to cutbacks, and, after her father's death, her mother had moved in with them, due to health issues. Suddenly, Allison felt like the weight of the world was crashing down on her. She had little time or money for counseling, but Allison knew she was in trouble when she began having panic attacks while riding in the elevator to the 12th floor of the building where she worked.

She felt and heard her heart beating so loudly that she thought that every day might be her last. Her thoughts raced. "What if I have a heart attack?" "What if my heart can't take this and gives out?" Knowing that her family depended on her, she somehow summoned up the courage to go on, even though she felt incredibly uncomfortable and weak. After a while, the panic attacks were no longer just on the elevator. They were happening while she drove to and from work, in her office, and even while she was on the phone. As she tried desperately to manage one anxiety, ten more surfaced. But, like many phobic people, she hid her struggles well.

No one knew the hell she was going through. Everyone depended on her, at home and at work. She was desperately trying to live up to her own expectations, as well as those of others.

Allison recognized that the panic attacks were probably due to extreme stress, but she also feared that she might be losing her mind. Each day she anticipated the panic attacks. Every morning, as she woke up, she set the stage for these horrible attacks, by thinking about, dreading, and expecting them, providing her fears the fuel to ignite yet another series of attacks. What you focus on, good or bad, will manifest itself, and Allison was, daily, feeding her fears.

## Santa and Sanity

The holidays were approaching and, with all the increased pressures, Allison was beginning to unravel. The cost of buying gifts and trying to find the time to shop, bake, and travel, seemed like mountains to climb. She awoke each morning feeling the stress in her belly, wondering how she would ever pull this off. She feared losing her job due to the panic attacks; she was afraid of losing her home if that happened. She imagined her entire family being put on the streets. Allison was worried that, if she didn't continue to work hard, she would be replaced, especially if they found out about her panic attacks and her fears that she was crazy.

A few nights before Christmas, the office held their traditional office party. Allison had always attended and was the one who pulled it all together. She baked each night the week before, as she had done for the past eight years, and brought in her plates of buttery delights for each person in the office, along with a personal note and a brightly-colored bow attached to their gifts. The office staff was thrilled and had come to expect her holiday treats. Allison did everything for everyone except for... Allison. At this Christmas party, Allison did something that she rarely did – she drank.

She drank white wine, because that was the only way she could calm herself. And, it worked. It worked too well.

She soon discovered that having a glass of wine before going home dulled her panicky feelings. She began having a small shot glass before bedtime and then a few sips in the morning, to keep her legs steady on the elevator. Then she tucked a tiny bottle in her purse, so that she could pour the liquid relaxer down her throat in the bathroom at the office. Allison carried lots of gum and breath fresheners to hide the familiar, sweet smell. She was very aware that she might be on her way to becoming an alcoholic, she just didn't know what to do so she could function each day.

Her family didn't know – no one did up until now.

She had gotten sick with strep throat and, during the visit with her doctor, she told him everything. They had a long relationship, and she trusted him. He asked her about her family and job and then remarked about the slight tremor he saw in her hands. Allison buried her face in her hands and began to sob. She blurted out everything. She expressed her fears of being institutionalized as well. He put his arm about her shoulders and began to tell her that there was help and hope. He discussed trying an anti-anxiety medication, and he handed her my name, scribbled on his prescription pad, along with an antibiotic for her strep throat, while telling her to take a week off. The office would go on without her. It was critical for Allison to take care of Allison.

*Just a note about my feelings toward medication:*

*There are great anti-anxiety medications out there now, and I strongly suggest that you discuss these with your doctor. However, they are not "magic pills" – even with them, you will still need to learn coping skills. Many people think it's a sign of weakness to be on such medication – it is not. If you and your physician decide that you need this help, by all means take it.*

Before Allison called me, I heard from her doctor, and I assured him that I would make time for her. We met the following week, and Allison was feeling cured of her strep throat, but the panic attacks were still a problem. She had stopped drinking. She didn't want to combine alcohol with antibiotics, and some of her panic had subsided because she did not need to get into the elevator and she was free from the pressures at work. She was fortunate that she didn't get addicted to the alcohol and that she was passionate about pursuing other methods to deal with her anxiety. In this case, her fears actually worked in her favor, because she was fearful of mixing medication with alcohol. But, she still had her pattern of getting up each morning and expecting and dreading the panic. She was welcoming these attacks into her life by "feeding" them with her thoughts. Expecting and dreading panic attacks will always fuel them. The first step is accepting them, and then moving forward.

When Allison walked into my office on a cold February afternoon, with her long dark hair and deep set brown eyes, I thought she resembled Catherine Zeta-Jones. I remember thinking how striking she was, and how people with phobias and fears can be so outwardly confident and gracious, while hiding the volcano of emotions erupting inside.

We spoke in length about her responsibilities at home, at work, and the tremendous amount of stress she was under as the family bread winner and caretaker of her mother. I then explained to her that I had her background history and her doctor did as well, and that we would not need to talk about it again. Our job was to get beyond that, to not get stuck in a blame game on the home-front or at work, but to show her how to move forward, to gain confidence, and to cut off the fears that were generating her panic attacks. If she also wanted to talk to a marriage counselor, psychologist, or psychiatrist, I was fine with that. But in my therapy sessions, we were going to stay in the present and begin starving off those fearful thoughts.

## It's Raining, It's Pouring... Tomatoes?

I explained to Allison that she had been holding all of her feelings in because she didn't want her husband to feel bad about losing his job, nor did she want her mother to feel guilty about living with them. She certainly didn't want to discuss her problems with friends or colleagues at the office, because she felt that she needed to be responsible both at home and at work. But, because she was not expressing them, her fears were welling up, causing a "rain barrel effect."

## What is a "rain barrel effect"?

If you've never heard of this before, you may find this useful, and it's such a great visual. One time, when I was experiencing allergy problems, a doctor who specializes in allergy treatments explained it to me this way:

A patient comes to the doctor with a rash, hives, or eyes swollen shut due to allergens. He tells the doctor that he ate a tomato sandwich, thus the tomatoes caused the reaction, and now he wants a shot so he can eat tomatoes again. The truth is, the tomato is not *the* culprit.

If this patient evaluated his current lifestyle, he would recognize that the pollen count was high and the weather warmer, so the windows in his home were open for the first time in months. This let in a rush of pollen, while the breeze kicked up the dust in the house. Then he washed the dog, adding extra dander to the home environment. He then vacuumed, which threw dust particles around, while the old vacuum bag emitted some molds into the air. Then, he stopped for lunch, and made a tomato sandwich and – voila! The man now has a big old rash, which he thinks is from eating a tomato. But, it is probably not. You see, this person's "rain barrel" (in this case his physical response to his environment) was filled with pollen, dander, dust, mold, etc. His body was like a rain barrel, filled with environmental triggers, and he was able to contain a response to it, until that tomato was tossed in. That did it! It began to spill over, and now there was a mess – hives, sneezing, and wheezing.

The principle is the same for anxiety attacks. In Allison's case, her panic attacks were a result of a myriad of stressful thoughts. The money, the job, the house, her mother, and on and on. Then, one day, she stepped into the elevator and felt the true meaning of feeling trapped. When the door closed, Allison found herself standing in a box, trapped, and pushed up against other people. Her emotional rain barrel overflowed, and her negative thoughts began to spiral out of control.

## White Coat Nightmares

The first things I taught Allison were relaxation techniques, which could be used to calm her mind. Breathing correctly is the key to immediately reducing, and even stopping, a panic attack (see breathing techniques in chapter 4). Over the next few visits, I used hypnotherapy to deeply relax her mind, and this enabled her to think more clearly. She learned to see things as they really were and to not view everything at catastrophic. This worked beautifully for her, as it does with most people.

Allison needed to know that she was okay. She needed assurance that she was not losing, or going to lose, her mind. The thought of being locked up in an institution, due to her inability to cope, terrified her. In Allison's mind, the picture was quite real and terrible. She pictured strong men in white coats carrying her out of her home, as she kicked and screamed, while duct tape was put over her mouth to silence her. She thought about them giving her an injection to put her to sleep – for good, she feared. This was just one of the visions playing over and over again in her mind. No wonder she was so exhausted and scared.

By using hypnosis techniques, I was able to harness Allison's highly creative and visual mind for her own good. I took her through positive visualizations, showing her how she could delegate some of her responsibilities to other family members. She practiced seeing and feeling people respond to her in a positive way – picturing them with smiles began a shift in her thinking. We did the same with her job. She worked at seeing and reenacting different scenarios in her mind, and creating the desired outcome seemed very feasible to her now. Guided imagery works very well. If your mind can see it, and you believe it, then you will act upon it.

## Imagine That!

Allison's fears began to diminish as she cut off their life-line. Over a period of just a few weeks, she spoke to her family and asked for help in the home, and, because she presented her position in such a positive way, not angry or accusatory, her husband, son, and mother were extremely supportive, and they came up with a variety of ways to take the pressure off of her. She was amazed! She had envisioned this conversation through guided imagery, and the end result was even better than she imagined. She did the same at work. She spoke with her boss about lightening her workload and explained that she was taking work home and working on the weekends. And again, she received not only support, but was given a raise and a part-time assistant. Her boss had no idea that Allison was so overworked, because she always carried the load without any complaint.

Allison soon found herself singing in the car on the way to work, and her panic attacks were gone. When she felt anxious, she would immediately belly breathe, using the alternate nostril technique (see Chapter 4), and then feed her mind positive thoughts, or look at photos that made her happy, or begin to hum a song. Diverting her mind and energy toward pleasant thoughts and emotions helped her to create a sense of peace and joy.

I still work with Allison, as she loves our hypnosis sessions. She comes to see me once or twice a month for her "tune up" and is enjoying life so much more. She has learned that what you don't feed, cannot live. She no longer lives with fearful thoughts, and she is continuing to use visualization techniques every day at home, helping her to create the life she desires- and you can too.

**Try this today:**

Close your eyes, and imagine how you'll look and feel when you're free of fears. Picture the smile on your face; imagine yourself visiting old friends, seeing new places, and venturing out. Hold that image, and feel the joy of being free.
Do this a few times every day, and you'll be amazed at what this small mental exercise can do for you.

*Only when we are no longer afraid do we begin to live.*

Dorothy Thompson

*Man's rise or fall, success or failure, happiness or unhappiness depends on his attitude... a man's attitude will create the situation he imagines.*

**James Lane Allen**

# CHAPTER VIII

# Matt's Story

## Matt's Story

Matt's mother phoned my office, to ask if I thought hypnosis sessions could help her 15 year old son, Matt, overcome anxiety. He was having problems in school, was fearful at home, and she noticed that he was no longer socializing with his core group of friends. She didn't see signs of depression, only that he had a few panic attacks and was now avoiding many situations. Because I had lived through those kinds of experiences at that age, I felt certain that I could help Matt.

A week later, Matt slinked into my office with his head hanging down. He had thick, black hair and a wiry frame, and I knew that this was the last place he wanted to be. He was very timid and quiet, and I don't think we ever made eye contact that day. He kept his head down and, when he did occasionally look up, his eyes darted around the room. I can only imagine what a 15 year old boy was thinking about *relaxation counseling* and hypnotherapy!

I first explained to him that true clinical hypnosis was nothing like what is shown on TV or in movies. And I told him that he would do only what he wanted to do, that he would not quack like a duck or howl at the moon. In fact, I explained he would feel much better than he has felt in a long time, just by taking control and learning how to relax. Hypnosis would not take away any power from him; it would give him his power back, in a much more positive way. As Matt listened, his hands stopped fidgeting. When he first sat down, he was white-knuckled and gripped the arms of the chair like he was on his first airplane flight.

I took Matt through a ten minute relaxation session, helping him to completely relax from head to toe. I had him use his imagination for his own good, so that he could see and feel that he, indeed, had the power to let go of his stress, to breathe more deeply, and to allow his body to feel loose and limp. He closed his eyes readily and tightly, his way of shutting out the world...and me. But, by the end of this brief ten minute relaxation/visualization session, when he opened his eyes, he looked relaxed and grateful. We had reached my goal for that visit.

We scheduled another appointment for the following week, and I felt certain Matt would keep it. Teenagers can be unpredictable, especially when mom is making the decision to see me, but something in Matt's eyes told me that he was willing to do more work to remove his demons.

## Devils, Demons and Darkness

When Matt came the next week, he walked in with his head down and still didn't make eye contact. The only difference was that he knew which office to go into and what chair to sit in, which he quickly did. After asking him a few questions about how he felt since our last meeting, he said that he felt great about the relaxation part but that he didn't want to talk. I knew that his inner self-talk was loud and scary, so my goal was to get him to do exactly what he didn't want to. I thought we might be in for a long-term relationship.

For a few weeks, I only worked with him on ways to relax, explaining visualization and the power of his words and thoughts over his life, and showing him how his body reacted to both stress and relaxation. Matt listened, but was awkwardly silent. I just didn't have a lot to go on.

During each of our sessions, his time in relaxation lengthened, and he easily took in long, deep breaths. I could tell that every part of his body was relaxed. But, I also felt that this was the only time he was feeling this way, and I couldn't figure out why he wasn't leaking out some information about his life and thoughts. His mother only knew that he had trouble sleeping, that he was not socializing like he used to, and that he had trouble focusing on school work.

Matt didn't seem seriously depressed. His family doctor, who had recently examined him, didn't feel he was either. But Matt seemed scared, and I couldn't put my finger on it. On Matt's next visit, I decided we would have a chat, even if I was the only one talking. For the first twenty minutes, I didn't turn on the soft music or dim the lights, the things he was used to before a relaxation session, and he seemed bewildered and anxious. I asked questions and he answered, with a polite "yes" or "no," until I asked him if he had seen any movies lately. Knowing that he hadn't been going out, I thought I'd hear a no. However, Matt's body jerked upright in the chair, and he said he wanted to see a movie called "Stigmata," but he could hardly look at the advertisements on TV because they scared him.

In fact, he was terrified of the movie - the thought of it and what it meant for him. He asked me if I had seen it. This was the first time he had asked me a question! I hadn't seen the movie, but I had seen the commercials, which seemed very demonic and quite scary. In fact, the movie's tag line was *"It will scare the hell out of you."*

Matt's face was ashen as he spoke and his dark eyes alive with fear. He said that he was afraid that it would happen to him. That his hands would bleed, that the Devil would possess his body, that God would not forgive him for his thoughts, for being afraid, for not being trusting. Matt's mind was brimming over with fearful thoughts and, now, I was finally able to hear them.

Matt grew up in a very religious, traditional, Catholic home. Similar to my own upbringing. He had been an altar boy at his local church, when he was younger, and believed in God and an afterlife. But Matt believed in a condemning, angry, and vengeful God. And he thought that his chances of getting into Heaven were extraordinarily slim. He thought only people like Mother Theresa went to heaven, and he thought he had no chance.

This movie brought all of Matt's fears to the surface. He was afraid of becoming possessed by the Devil, and he felt he would never be good enough for God. He thought he always fell short in God's eyes. He was sure that he would spend an eternity in hell and was constantly afraid of dying. *Stigmata* was one of the latest movies focusing on this subject, and it was hitting him at a very vulnerable age. But Matt had seen a lot of movies like this one, such as *The Exorcist*, etc. These movies, combined with the intense focus he put on them, literally became his "bibles of fear."

## Truth Verses Hollywood

With this knowledge, I could begin to help Matt get to the core of his fears and choke off those strongholds of fear. Jesus said, "You shall know the truth, and the truth shall make you free." It was time to free Matt.

The following week, Matt walked in with a smile, a look between old friends now, as we began to share some thoughts and secrets. This was a real breakthrough. On the small table between us, I placed two bibles. Ironically, Matt had never read the Bible. He knew the church rituals, basic prayers, the story of Christ, the Christmas and Easter stories, and that was all. I told Matt that if he was going to believe Hollywood's version of God and demons, why not go to the main source? And, that's what we did; we began reading together from the New Testament, using the amplified version, which made the content easier to read and more lively for him.

Matt was amazed at the teachings of Christ. He read Jesus' words, *"I say emphatically that anyone who listens to my message and believes in God who sent me has eternal life, and will never be damned for his sins, but has already passed out of death and into life"* from the book of John. In the book of Mark, "If you only have faith in God – this is the absolute truth – you can say to this Mount of Olives, *'Rise up and fall into the*

*Mediterranean' and your command will be obeyed. All that's required is that you really believe and have no doubt."* I could see a change beginning in Matt. He read as though he were feeding a hunger deep inside of him. The words were changing his thinking. And his new thoughts were healing him. It was fascinating to watch, and humbling to be part of this awakening.

*Everything that Matt was living in fear of, existed in Hollywood's version of sensational movie-making. And sensationalism sells tickets.*

I wanted Matt to read and understand what his faith was based on, the teachings of Jesus Christ. Jesus preached love, forgiveness, and eternal life. In fact, the Devil had very little to do with it, and Jesus makes it quite clear that there was victory over the evil by staying close to Him and just believing.

Matt was quickly seeing that he was far more powerful because of his faith. That God loved him and was not condemning him at every turn of the road. He beamed when he read out loud from the book of John: *"For God loved the world so much that He gave His only Son so that anyone* who believes in Him shall not perish but have eternal life. God did not send His Son into the world to condemn it, but to save it." And he was greatly comforted by St. Paul's words in his letter to the Philippians, where he is quoted as saying: *"Don't worry about anything, instead pray about everything: Tell God your needs and don't forget to thank him for his answers. If you do this you will experience God's peace, which is far more wonderful than the human mind can understand. His peace will keep your thoughts and our hearts quiet and at rest as you trust in Christ Jesus. Fix your thoughts on what is true and good and right. Think about things that are pure and lovely, and dwell on the fine, good things in others. Think about all you can praise God for and be glad about. Keep putting into practice all you learned from me and saw me doing, and the God of peace will be with you."*

That was it! Matt's mind took a major turn at this point, and a real healing took place as he began to focus on the positive messages of God. He began to feel good about himself and his future; he joined the dance of life again. It was inspiring to see that anxious, fearful boy turn into a happy and peaceful being, right in front of my eyes.

## Matt's Story

Matt's mom wrote to me a few months after our sessions ended, thanking me for helping her son. She was very grateful and thrilled for his recovery. Did I do anything? Not really. I just steered him in the right direction and helped him back on the track he was meant to be traveling in life.

*Words which do not give the light of Christ
increase the darkness.*

**Mother Teresa**

*If you knew who walked beside you at all times on this path that you have chosen, you would never experience fear or doubt again.*

**From "A Course in Miracles"**

# CHAPTER IX

# Emily's Story

## Emily's Story

When Emily first phoned me, she could not leave her home. There was no way that she could come into the office. She was agoraphobic and only ventured out when she absolutely had to see a doctor, and even then she needed about 5 – 10 mg of Valium to tackle the anxiety.

Someone told her about me and the success that I was having with those suffering with panic attacks, even full blown agoraphobia. Because I had been through it myself, she felt that I could be the one to help her out of her "pit of hell," as she called it.

I was quite surprised when I met her. Emily was stunningly beautiful, with long, blonde hair, a girlish figure, and blue eyes that sparkled when she greeted me at her door. Frankly, many homebound people that I have worked with did not have the pizzazz that Emily emoted.

However, I quickly found that this was as good as it got for her.

She was married to a very loving and kind man, who seemed strangely comfortable in Emily's small world. The partner of an agoraphobic can suffer just as much, because the world changes for them as well. Emily and her husband could not do simple things together as a couple. They couldn't dine out or visit friends, and traveling was out of the question. I noticed a gorgeous photo of Emily on her wedding day and photos of a honeymoon in Aruba many years ago, so, obviously, they had had a life before the agoraphobia took over. Did he feel robbed? I know that Emily did!

We began by talking about anything and everything, as I wanted to get a feel for Emily's fears and I wanted her to trust me. She had been through so many counselors, and I knew only too well how exhausting that could be. She told me that this was her last attempt for getting help. Wow, talk about pressure!

After several sessions with me as the driver, Emily felt comfortable enough to take a very short drive with me- just one block. This took all of the courage she could muster. We then mapped out a plan. I would pick her up every Sunday and we would take this drive, extending the distance a little bit each time. Within a month, just four visits and drives, Emily was at the wheel. We drove into town- the first time for her in years. She was exhilarated! She did it! The following week, we got out of the car and went into a Dunkin Donuts. She sat, with her eyes gleaming, and sipping her decaffeinated coffee, while looking around at everything with new eyes.

She still feared having a panic attack and was always expecting panic to creep up and grab her. I hoped she would have one. The only way she would break away from her safety zone was by knowing that she could handle this extreme anxiety, no matter where she was. Uncomfortable? You bet, but it would subside. We worked on breathing techniques and the tools needed to pull herself out of a state of panic, when and if that would happen.

But only when Emily could accept that it would occur, and have faith that she could starve the attack by not feeding it, would she truly be able to overcome it. However, Emily still hoped that she would never experience a panic attack in public, which kept her limited to small jaunts away from her home.

## The Big Day

After two months of sessions, Emily decided she wanted to try driving to the next town, which was 20 miles away. This was a huge step for her. She put her rosary beads in one pocket and a lucky stone with the word "calm" written on it in the other, along with her grandmother's handkerchief and lots of gum to chew to distract herself. She donned a pair of very large and dark sunglasses. When anxiety kicks in, things can appear much brighter than usual. Plus, the sunglasses provided a little shield to hide behind.

The trip began surprisingly uneventfully, as I watched her breathing easily, while concentrating on the road. I kept in mind that she had not done this in about 15 years. As soon as we crossed into the next town, she let out a gasp of excitement, which quickly began to turn into an anxious feeling for her. Excitement and anxiety are two emotions that are very much alike. Some people say, "Oh, boy!" when they're excited, while those prone to anxiety/panic often say "Oh, no!" Feelings can quickly become very intense, which is often associated with feeling out-of-control and unstable. I reminded Emily to close her mouth and to breathe through her nostrils, which automatically sends a message to her brain that she's ok. Diaphragmatic breathing is key, and it's the quickest way out of a panic attack. By breathing through her nostrils instead of gulping air through her mouth, Emily began to relax. Her anxiety level lowered, and she was able to maneuver the car into a parking lot adjoining a women's clothing store. Emily had not shopped for herself in many years, and I was excited for her to finally have the chance to do it.

The store was overwhelming to her – so many colors, stacks of apparel, the lights are bright, and women are bustling about. We hung out at the front of the store at first. She wanted to retreat, but I reminded her that leaving early defeated the purpose. It was important for her to confront her fear, pass through it, and move on. I told her to concentrate on one table of winter scarves and gloves. To stay in the moment, feel the fabric, look at the colors – and to slowly breathe. She did so beautifully, and she purchased a pair of gloves.

Standing in line and waiting to pay can feel claustrophobic, as it can be very, very anxiety producing. You have to pay- you can't leave the store without doing so or you'll be arrested, and there's a sense of feeling trapped. Emily didn't have to wait in any lines for years. Her mother bought most of her clothes, and her husband did all of the grocery shopping. Being in new territory can be frightening or exhilarating, but for Emily these emotions were scary. After successfully purchasing her gloves, Emily was exhausted. But she still had a 20 mile drive home.

Carefully getting behind the steering wheel, Emily said she couldn't do it. "Yes, you can," I firmly told her. We sat for a while, and I knew she was upset. I asked her to use her tools to get her through.

She pursed her lips together and took a few long breaths via her nostrils, resting her head back onto the head-rest. She pulled out her smooth stone, with the word "calm" written on it, and gave it a squeeze. She then looked at me and said, "Let's go." We made the same trip the following week.

The next week, I sat in the backseat and Emily was alone upfront. The week after that, I again sat in the backseat, but we didn't speak. Emily was preparing herself for driving alone, for the first time in nearly 18 years. She put on music and was driving with ease. I think she forgot that I was in the backseat. It was lovely to watch.

## Going the Distance

Emily was now shopping with ease. She had learned how to successfully deal with panic attacks, and her fear of her fear was leaving her. I wanted her husband to join us on our little trips, so that I could guide him on helping her, too, as he was the one she was mainly with. However, I noticed that when her husband was with her, she became more fearful. Not of him, but she allowed her fear to take over more quickly than she did when we were alone. She reverted to a childlike state as he told her that he would drive, that he would go into the store, that she should take a week off from driving, as she was too tired.  I sensed that he was afraid of losing her, and that he had become very comfortable with his beautiful wife staying at home with him.

Emily was not able to have children and had created a warm and inviting home.  She was an excellent cook.  This was her world – nothing beyond this, except for escaping by reading travel books.  She so wanted to travel, but when you can't go beyond your mailbox without having a major anxiety attack, this seemed impossible.  Until now.  Now, Emily was actually thinking about hopping a plane.

In my field of work, it has been my experience to see that most agoraphobics are adventurous at heart.  They are bright and bold and want to explore.  They are limited by their own fears and when they know how to live without the fear of their fears, they truly live and enjoy life! They really know how to enjoy life.  As I watched  Emily come out of her cocoon, I could also feel her husband's fear.

After several months, Emily no longer needed my services.  She was doing her own shopping, driving to her own doctor's appointments, and visiting her mother, and she was thinking about taking a course in real estate. Her face was as vibrant out of her "safe space" as it was when I first met her at her home. The world was becoming her "safe space," and that's exactly the way it should be.

Emily and I have been in contact, on and off, for many years. We attended a concert together, and she drove from Connecticut to Massachusetts. We had a great time, and she looked like a million bucks. This woman, who could not drive alone for one block, was amazing me with stories of driving to Newport, RI, where she drove over huge, high bridges that many people have trouble crossing, even though they don't have phobias or panic attacks. She has been on several trips to various states with her husband, on a plane.

Emily now lives in San Diego, where she is a real estate broker with her own agency. Her husband runs the business with her and has a new respect for her and a new life as well. I am so proud of this woman! Emily learned to never let her fears grow – she starved them by not feeding them.

By simply confronting her fears and moving forward, and accepting that she would feel uncomfortable, she starved them out of her life.

ooooo

*What you don't feed will fade away.*

*What will your life look like if you lived it fearlessly? Write it down and believe that you can have the life that you desire!*

_____
_____
_____
_____
_____
_____
_____
_____
_____
_____
_____
_____
_____
_____
_____
_____
_____
_____
_____
_____
_____
_____
_____
_____
_____
_____
_____
_____
_____
_____
_____
_____

*You gain strength, courage and confidence by every experience in which you really stop to look fear in the face. You are able to say to yourself, 'I have lived through this horror. I can take the next thing that comes along.' You must do the thing you think you cannot do.*

**Eleanor Roosevelt**

# CHAPTER X

# What My Mother Taught Me

## What My Mother Taught Me

My mother, Ann, was beautiful, bright, and charming. She raised three children, while keeping her home filled with homemade treats and loads of friends. Flexing her culinary muscles, she created everything from flamboyant six-layer cakes to her own version of a gourmet pizza- and, back in the 50's, who ever heard of "gourmet pizza"? At her funeral service, her friends spoke of her Friday night pizzas, and their now-grown children told of walking miles each week, just so they could enjoy her food and friendship.

As a child, I remember lying in bed many nights, hearing whispers from relatives and family friends, softly crying at our kitchen table as they spoke of their problems, which my mother would soothe over a cup of coffee, along with something she had made that morning. She called this time "coffee and," as pearls of wisdom flew out of her mouth and were eagerly soaked up by the wounded at our table.

Naturally, I didn't quite understand what was happening. Only that people seemed to flock to her, and sometimes they were sad, and, somehow, my mom made it better for them.

Little did any of us know that my mother's world was very small. She did not venture out much and never, ever on her own. She lost herself in baking, cleaning, and being with her family and friends at home. Whether speaking on the phone or in person, people were drawn to her. Yet, my mother had no one to confide in about her own pain. In her day, you wouldn't dare speak of "nervous problems," for fear that you'd be locked up. I know now that this was my mother's biggest fear. She was very claustrophobic and feared if others knew what she couldn't do and how her nerves felt raw at times, she would be deemed "insane" and locked away. The thought of that was like being buried alive, and she was tortured by it, keeping it well hidden.

She simply entertained in her home and went out with my dad, and at least one of us kids, on Sunday afternoon drives, which usually required her to use a prescription tranquilizer. The thought of being left home alone, while my dad took us out, resulted in waves of panic attacks.

She would later tell me that she had to choose "the lesser of two evils," between the car ride or being alone. And staying alone was just not an option for her. I realize now that, by distracting herself with others and her obsessive culinary interests, she was saving her mind and her life.

Of course she could help others – she was going through some of the same issues, or dealing with even worse things inside her head. She knew how to lead others out, but she could not help herself out of the trenches of fear and panic.

*Only when I developed my own fears, did Mom confide in me.*

*I knew she felt guilty about passing on her fears to me but she also wondered who she had gotten her fears from.*

Did she have pearls of wisdom for me? You bet she did!

She gave me books written by Norman Vincent Peale, on the "Power of Positive Thinking." She told me to face my fears now or I'd get a thousand more. She told me not to think so much about them, to change the way I thought, and... to watch the Andy Griffith show on TV. Andy Griffith? Yes. She found his show to be relaxing and thought that he had a calming effect.

There is a lot to be said for that!

I must say watching that show was probably the best advice she gave me!

I still highly recommend watching Andy's show for anyone who needs to relax; it's in syndication and will be around for many years to come, I hope! It's a far cry from what we're barraged with today. Doesn't sitting on Andy's porch in Mayberry, with a piece of Aunt Bee's peach pie, sound wonderful? It sure beats watching the news today!

But, the biggest lesson my mother taught me came after she suffered a heart attack. Just about everything she had ever feared happened to her. She was out of her safety zone and potentially facing death. No family members could stay overnight with her, and everything seemed startling, strange, and frightening. I truly felt that this would be the end for my mom. But then, something happened that no one expected. She told us that if she made it through this, she could make it through anything.

That she had made up her mind to simply enjoy life and to live fearlessly. She was determined to put all that she's ever read into action.

But could she really do it? Or was she just fooling herself to get through this? We wouldn't know till she got home and back on her feet.

## A New Life

Mom came home. Following her doctor's orders to a T, she began walking every day. This was something I had not seen in my lifetime. Mom never walked alone. At first, she went to the end of our driveway, then down the street, and, eventually, she was walking one mile a day. Walking, waving to neighbors, and smiling like she truly enjoyed it. This was all so foreign to her family.

The shocker was yet to come. My mother began losing weight, due to her new way of eating. She was preparing recipes now from the "American Heart Association Diet," instead of the butter and cheese laden recipes from TV Guide, or cheesecake recipes from the inside of

Philadelphia Cream Cheese wrappings. Feeling this new confidence in herself, and staying true to her words in the hospital, my mother booked a flight for her and my dad to Las Vegas. My mother had never flown before. She made arrangements through a local travel agency, and my parents became part of a junket to Vegas. We were completely stunned!

My father was thrilled. He was a hardworking gas station owner, or "grease monkey," as he would often say. He always dreamed of traveling. But no one was certain if she would really go through with the trip. We didn't know this new person that my mother had become.

But, they took the trip, and my mother had a blast. It was exhilarating to see the photos of her on the plane, with a cocktail in hand, happily walking around and snapping photos of her own. Years later, after she died, I was cleaning out her apartment and found photos of her that she had never shared with the family. They were sweet photos that my dad took, probably on their second trip to Vegas (yes, they went again), and she had a lovely peignoir on. She looked like a new bride.

Only then did I realize what a gift she had been given. Finally, she truly was enjoying life. She wasn't listening to others at her kitchen table as much, she was no longer distracting herself with food, and she jumped into life! She was truly living life for the first time, in over 30 years. She tossed caution to the wind that day in the hospital, looked fear straight in the face, and said "Enough!" That made me realize that it's both as simple and as difficult as that.

**She starved her fears away.**

I did not want to have a heart attack to get that message. Nor have anything else earth-shattering happen to make me begin accepting my fears, thereby killing them off.

Jesus is quoted as saying: "Faith without works is dead." How true that is. All those wonderful books my mother had read and passed on to me did absolutely nothing for us because, although we read them and intellectually understood the lessons, we never put the information into action.

You can read this book, or any other book on overcoming fears, until you can recite it to others, and you too can become a "kitchen counselor," or an authority on the subject. But, until you take that leap of faith and apply action, you'll never move beyond it. My mother's unbridled fearlessness inspired me and still inspires me. I will forever remember to face my fears, and they will pass away. The severity will not last. The heart racing, thought racing, all of that - will pass.

This woman, my "new mother," who could not drive alone nor be home alone, became a gad about! I would call her, and many times my dad would answer, saying that she was out "gallivanting around." She drove over bridges, out to malls, visiting her sisters-in-law, and, till the day she died, she drove every day and everywhere. Ironically, she became the person who drove others around. She loved her freedom; the world was hers. She was able to work, travel, and enjoy life...you can't put a price on that!

She feared life for a good part of her life, but once she "got it" she dug in and just did it; she had 30 more years of fearless living. She passed away at 85 and drove to visit friends right till the end.

## If she can do it – you can too!

The more you get out there and say "I can do this" – and know that it's okay to feel uncomfortable – the more you, too, will find your life enjoyable and fulfilling. It's yours right now, and it's just a thought and action away!

*My mom personifies overcoming fears with just a change of her thought patterns. She is beaming with joy as she boards a plane, with my dad, for the first time in her life! She is my hero. Let her inspire you too!*

*I am not afraid of storms, for I am learning how to sail my ship.*

**Louisa May Alcott**

*What you think about expands into all areas of your life: May your thoughts be laser focused on happier outcomes and you'll find that joy will begin to creep in and fill those negative places. That's a promise.*

*Life is short; enjoy every moment!*
*Written for you with love,*

**Joyce Logan**

Made in the USA
Monee, IL
10 June 2026

52191935R00115